KINS   DUNCAN   C.BELL   MOTHELL   McCALL   DRAKE   SWEATT   WILKINSON   DR.SMITH   SPEDDER

A Negro League Scrapbook

A Negro League Scrapbook

Carole Boston Weatherford

Foreword by Buck O'Neil

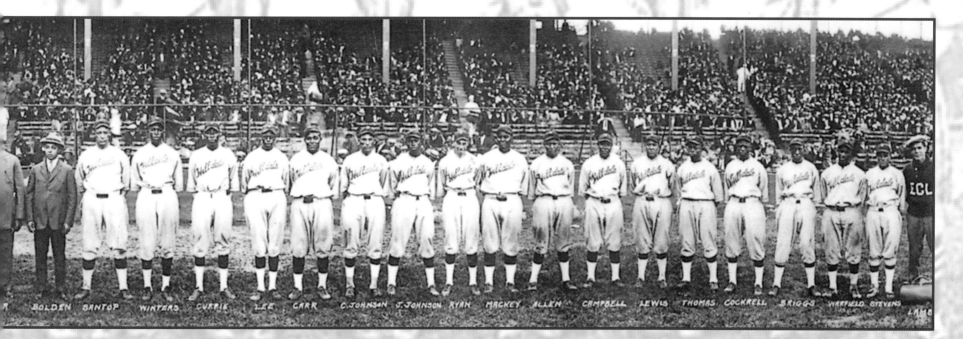

BOLDEN SANTOP WINTERS CURRIE LEE CARR C. JOHNSON J. JOHNSON RYAN MACKEY ALLEN CAMPBELL LEWIS THOMAS COCKRELL BRIGGS WARFIELD STEVENS

Boyds Mills Press
Honesdale, Pennsylvania

The author is grateful to have received assistance from Bill Burdick of the National Baseball Hall of Fame Library, Professor Lawrence Hogan of Union County College, Larry Lester of NetNoir Research, and Buck O'Neil, chairman of the Negro Leagues Baseball Museum.

Picture research was partially funded by a Central Piedmont Regional Artist Hub Grant from the North Carolina Arts Council.

Boyds Mills Press, Inc.
815 Church Street
Honesdale, Pennsylvania 18431
Printed in China

Library of Congress Cataloging-in-Publication Data

Weatherford, Carole Boston, 1956–
  A Negro league scrapbook / by Carole Boston
Weatherford.— 1st ed.
      p. cm.
ISBN 978-1-59078-091-6 (alk. paper)
1. Negro leagues—History. 2. Negro leagues—
History—Pictorial works. I. Title.
GV875.N35W43 2005
796.357'64'08996073—dc22
      2004019324

The text of this book is set in 11-point Caxton Book.

First edition

10 9 8 7 6 5 4 3

Photo Credits

For the heroic athletes who fought—and still fight—to level the playing field

—C. B. W.

Foreword

When I was a kid, all the towns had baseball teams. Everybody played the game. White kids dreamed of playing Major League baseball, and black kids dreamed of joining the Negro Leagues. For black kids, baseball was a way out of poverty.

I was from Florida, and I couldn't attend Sarasota High School or the University of Florida because they didn't admit blacks. But I could play baseball. I began playing with the Negro Leagues when I was twenty-five years old. I started with the Memphis Red Sox and joined the Kansas City Monarchs in 1938.

Negro League baseball was outstanding. At the time, the best black athletes played Negro League baseball, which was the third-largest black-owned business in the country. All you needed was a bus and a couple of sets of uniforms and you could have a great team.

Negro League teams trained in college towns. During training season, we played the college teams. And in the summer when school was out, college players and schoolteachers joined our teams. Forty percent of Negro League ballplayers were college men, compared with one percent of Major League players.

When the Negro Leagues started, teams rode the train. But that wasn't practical because the team had to go where the train went. With our own bus, we could play in towns where the trains didn't stop. We rode in some of the best buses that money could buy. In big cities, we stayed in the same hotels where all the black musicians and celebrities stayed. It was exciting. We'd play at Yankee Stadium before a crowd of 40,000 and stay in Harlem at the Hotel Woodside.

Kansas City Monarch manager Buck O'Neil in the dugout

6

At night, we'd go to hear Count Basie or another jazz band at the Apollo Theater. Sometimes I almost forgot about segregation.

Exhibition games against Major League teams gave people a chance to see Negro League baseball at its best. Negro League teams won most of those ball games because we had something to prove. We stretched that single into a double, that double into a triple, and we stole home. We showed that we could achieve on the playing field and in society.

Segregation was the only reason the Negro Leagues existed. When the Brooklyn Dodgers signed Jackie Robinson, that was really the beginning of the civil-rights movement. Baseball fans got a chance to see that black people could compete. That changed the way that black people were viewed in America.

This tribute to great athletes tells not only the story of the Negro Leagues but also the story of the United States during the segregation era. This history attests to how far we have come.

Buck O'Neil

John Jordan "Buck" O'Neil
Chairman, Negro Leagues Baseball Museum
Kansas City, Missouri

"**There were**
and m

—Leroy R

8

nany **Satchels,**
any **Joshes.** "

bert **"Satchel" Paige**

Major League bans black and brown.
Negro leagues, a proving ground.

The Page Fence Giants, sponsored by the Page Woven Wire Fence Company of Adrian, Michigan, played between 1894 and 1898.

CUBAN GIANTS
BASE ★ BALL ★ CLUB.
SEASON TICKET 1887.
Admit _Wm Hy Beable_
NOT TRANSFERABLE.
S. K. Govern
_Mg'r_

A ticket to the Cuban Giants' 1887 championship season

Black Out

In 1887 the owners of all major league ball clubs agreed not to sign any more black players. Minor league owners followed suit. Determined to play professional ball, African Americans formed their own teams, beginning with the Cuban Giants in 1887. All-black teams prepared black players for the day that the major league would once again allow African Americans onto the field.

The Cuban Giants, originally from Long Island, New York, eventually settled in St. Augustine, Florida. This photo shows the team in 1887.

The Morris Brown College baseball team (circa 1900): Morris Brown College, located in Atlanta, Georgia, was founded in 1887 for the education of African American men and women.

Monarchs, Barons, Giants, Grays, All-black baseball's glory days.

The Chicago American Giants (1920–1931) were owned and managed by famed pitcher Andrew "Rube" Foster, seen here in suit. Foster was inducted into the Baseball Hall of Fame in 1981.

DETROIT STARS—1920

The Detroit Stars (1920–1933, 1937): This outstanding team, shown here in 1920, played for fifteen seasons.

TELEPHONE DOUGLAS 6059

BASE BALL COMMISSION
A. R. FOSTER, Chairman
JOHN T. BLOUNT
C. I. TAYLOR
J. L. WILKINSON

CABLE ADDRESS "RUBEFOS"

BOARD OF DIRECTORS
A. R. FOSTER, Chairman
T. W. CHAMPION
JOE GREEN
C. I. TAYLOR

National Association

Colored Professional Base Ball Clubs

WE ARE THE SHIP   ALL ELSE THE SEA

DETROIT STARS

TAYLOR'S A. B. C's.

KANSAS CITY MONARCHS

CINCINNATI (CUBAN STARS)

BASEBALL WESTERN BOOKING AGENCY BUREAU

AMERICAN GIANTS

CHICAGO GIANTS

ST. LOUIS GIANTS

COLUMBUS (BUCKEYES)

OPERATING THE NEGRO   NATIONAL LEAGUE, INC.

BACHARACH GIANTS, NEW YORK AND HILDALE, DARBY, PA., ASSOCIATED MEMBERS

BALTIMORE ELITE GIANTS

The Negro National League's first business card

The 1922 Kansas City Monarchs

Negro League Teams

The Negro National League was organized in 1919 by Andrew "Rube" Foster. It folded in 1931 and was revived in 1933 by Gus Greenlee. The Eastern Colored League, formed by white businessmen, operated from 1922 to 1928. H. G. Hall organized the Negro American League in 1937. The leagues included these teams:

Kansas City Monarchs
Indianapolis ABCs
Dayton Marcos
Chicago American Giants
Detroit Stars
St. Louis Giants
Cuban Giants
Pittsburgh Crawfords
Philadelphia Hilldales
Brooklyn Royal Giants
Lincoln Giants
Atlantic City Bacharachs
New York Cuban All-Stars
Columbus Blue Birds
Baltimore Black Sox
Nashville (late Baltimore) Elite Giants
New York Black Yankees
Newark Eagles
Cincinnati Tigers
Memphis Red Sox
Birmingham Black Barons
St. Louis Stars
Indianapolis Athletics

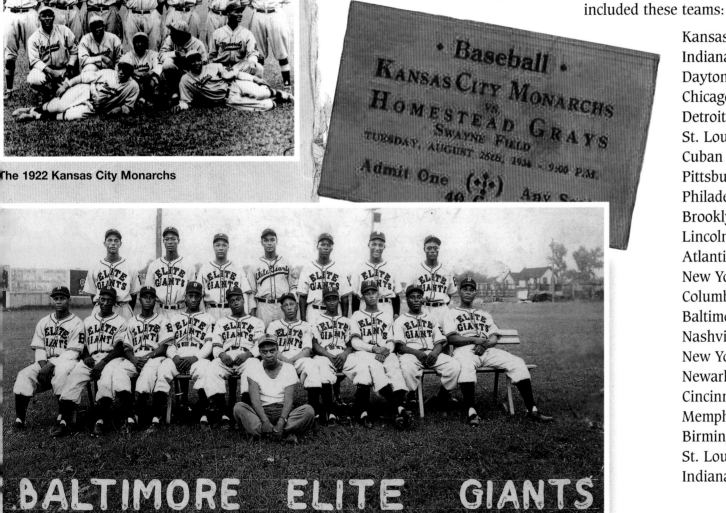
Baltimore Elite Giants

Faithful fans step out in style; Picnic baskets zigzag aisles.

A group of nattily dressed women at the ballgame. Sunday games were the social event of the week in the black community.

A crowd of 18,205 people attended the May 24, 1953, game between the Monarchs and the Clowns in Kansas City.

Picnic at the Ballpark

Negro League baseball games were both sports events and social occasions. Fans, dressed in their Sunday best, flocked to ballparks to see and be seen. For home games, many Negro League teams rented major or minor league ballparks. However, the concessions at those stadiums sometimes remained closed during Negro League games. So fans packed picnics.

BaseBall · BaseBall · BaseBall

EVERY SUNDAY

World Colored Champions

LINCOLN GIANTS

Plays Big Double Header at their Home Ground

PROTECTORY OVAL

East Tremont Ave.   Near 180th Street

Mgr. JOE WILLIAMS

NOTICE TO THE FANS

Take any Bronx Subway to East 177th Street and change to Westchester car going East

Coolest Ball Park in New York

Shaded Trees all around Grandstand and Bleachers

Music in Between Innings

A broadside from around 1918 for Lincoln Giants games at the Catholic Protectory in New York

Long, lean Satchel, bag of tricks.
Bee balls buzzing, strike out six.

Satchel Paige: Among the pitches for which he was famous was his overpowering fastball.

"Just take the ball and throw it where you want to. Throw strikes. Home plate don't move."

—Satchel Paige

Paige's Signature Pitches

Bee-ball	Hurry-up ball
Jump-ball	Bat dodger
Trouble-ball	Long Tom
Blooper	Little Tom
Screwball	Midnight rider
Wobbly ball	Four-day creeper
Whipsy-dipsy-do	Hesitation pitch

Leroy "Satchel" Paige was the Negro League's highest-paid player and one of baseball's greatest pitchers. With a slow windmill wind-up and a blazing fastball, he racked up 2,100 wins, 300 shutouts, and 55 no-hitters, and played for more than 250 teams. He once struck out twenty-four batters in a game. Paige had thirty different pitches and named each one. He was in his forties when he joined the Major League's Cleveland Indians in 1948.

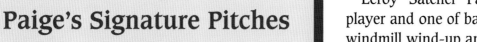

Satchel Paige toured with his All Stars in his own plane.

Smokey Joe's a pitching power, Hurls at ninety miles an hour.

Willie Foster

Leon Day

Smokey Joe Wiliams had other nicknames: "Cyclone" and "Strikeout."

18

Hilton Smith

"*We had a lot of Satchel Paiges out there—men who could throw the ball as hard as me. Ain't no maybe so about it.*"

—Satchel Paige

Rube Foster

Power Pitchers

"Satchel" Paige
  42 wins and 402 strikeouts in 1936

"Smokey Joe" Williams
  Catchers' hands swelled from his
    pounding pitches.
  41 wins and three losses in 1914

Wilbur "Bullet Joe" Rogan
  His fastballs zoomed past batters.

Andrew "Rube" Foster
  51 wins in 1902

"Cannonball" Dick Redding
  32 wins in 1929
  346 strikeouts in 1930

Willie Foster
  The Negro League's best left-handed pitcher

Hilton Smith
  Paige's relief pitcher and the league's best curve ball
  161 wins, 22 losses

Leon Day
  A wicked curve ball and a 95-mile-an-hour fastball

Strong Josh Gibson slugs, then sprints. Homer soars way past the fence.

The Pittsburgh Crawfords

Joshua "Josh" Gibson

HOMESTEAD GRAYS

Why was Josh Gibson called "the black Babe Ruth"?

Josh Gibson (1911–1947), a catcher for the Homestead Grays and Pittsburgh Crawfords, was one of the greatest power hitters in baseball history. He hit seventy-five home runs in 1931, sixty-nine in 1934, and led the Negro National League in home runs ten times. He once hit a homer about 580 feet, among the longest ever at Yankee Stadium. And folks say that one of his home run balls shattered a wooden seat in the stadium's grandstand.

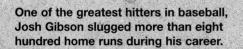
One of the greatest hitters in baseball, Josh Gibson slugged more than eight hundred home runs during his career.

Josh Gibson talking baseball with his young fans

Bullet Joe blasts a long line drive.
Spot Poles snares it, daring dive.

Wilbur "Bullet Joe" Rogan

Spot Poles: A powerful hitter, he took a leave from baseball at the height of his career to serve with the 369th Infantry in World War I. He was awarded five battle stars and a Purple Heart.

A fast, exciting game, Negro League baseball thrilled fans with crafty pitches, frequent bunts, hit-and-run plays, and stolen bases. Pitches illegal in the major league—spitters, shine balls, emery balls, darkened dirt balls, and knockdown pitches—were fair game in the Negro League. And some teams fined players who were tagged out standing up rather than sliding to base.

John Jordan "Buck" O'Neil played from 1927 to 1955 as a player and manager.

Cool, Cool Papa swats a fly,
Then like lightning flashes by.

Cool Papa Bell had extraordinary speed. He estimated that he had stolen around 175 bases in one season.

A centerfielder, Bell was so fast that he could rush in from the outfield to tag a runner at second base.

How fast was James "Cool Papa" Bell?

The story goes . . . Cool Papa could make it from first base to third on a bunt. He hit a ground ball and the ball hit him as he slid into second base. During a 1936 pregame exhibition, Olympic track and field champion Jesse Owens refused to race Bell around the bases. Supposedly, Bell could turn out the light in a room and be in bed before the room got dark. By all accounts, outfielder James "Cool Papa" Bell was the fastest runner in the Negro Leagues.

James Bell was known for his composure under pressure, hence his nickname.

The great player was inducted into the Baseball Hall of Fame in 1974.

George Mule Suttles, set to kick, Slams that curve ball hard and quick.

Willie "The Devil" Wells

Willie "The Devil" Wells

George "Mule" Suttles

Power Hitters

John Henry "Pop" Lloyd
Hit .418 in 1923; .444 in 1924;
4,005 career hits

Oscar Charleston (a.k.a. "the black
Ty Cobb," after baseball's first
Hall of Famer)
3,377 hits; .376 career batting average for league play

Walter "Buck" Leonard (a.k.a. "the black Lou Gehrig" after the
New York Yankees first baseman)
3,506 hits; .341 career batting average for league play

Ray Dandridge
.355 career batting average for league play

George "Mule" Suttles
.433 career batting average for league play

Louis Santop
.406 career batting average for league play

Norman "Turkey" Stearnes
Won league batting title four times in 1920s
Chosen for the 1933, 1934, 1935, and 1937 all-star teams

William Julius "Judy" Johnson (a.k.a. Mr. Sunshine)
.341 batting average for the first Negro World Series of 1924

Willie "The Devil" Wells
The league's best shortstop
Eight nominations to the East-West Game

Louis Santop

Oscar Charleston

Norman "Turkey" Stearnes

Walter "Buck" Leonard

John Henry "Pop" Lloyd

William Julius "Judy" Johnson

Double Duty minds the plate,
Tags a runner running late.

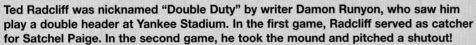

Martin Dihigo played every position on the field, and exceptionally so. He was inducted into the Hall of Fame in 1977.

Ted Radcliff was nicknamed "Double Duty" by writer Damon Runyon, who saw him play a double header at Yankee Stadium. In the first game, Radcliff served as catcher for Satchel Paige. In the second game, he took the mound and pitched a shutout!

N.Y. BLACK YANK

A player/manager, Jose Mendez won three straight National Negro League pennants with the Kansas City Monarchs, 1923–1925.

Double Trouble and Triple Threats

Due to tight budgets, Negro league team rosters were smaller than those of major league clubs. Luckily, some black players could hit, run, and field and excelled at more than one position. Ted "Double Duty" Radcliff was an all-star catcher and pitcher. Slugger George "Mule" Suttles played first base and outfield. Fastball pitcher "Bullet" Joe Rogan batted cleanup and played every position but catcher. Star pitcher Martin Dihigo could hit and play infield or outfield. Pitcher Jose Mendez also played infield. Known as utility players, these men played where they were needed.

Josh Gibson and Ted Radcliff meet at home plate.

Fans delight in thrills and laughs, High jinks, handshakes, autographs.

Lloyd "Pepper" Bassett—in his trademark rocking chair—played from 1934 to 1954.

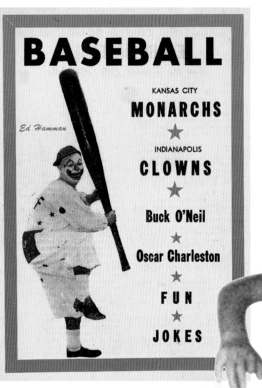

Despite on-the-field antics, the Indianapolis Clowns was a solid ball club.

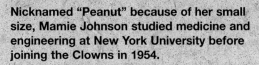

Nicknamed "Peanut" because of her small size, Mamie Johnson studied medicine and engineering at New York University before joining the Clowns in 1954.

Gags, Gals, and Clowns

Baseball was big-time entertainment. Some teams hired clowns and enlisted celebrities as umpires, honorary team captains, pinch hitters, or to throw out the first ball. Players also staged gags. Sitting in a rocking chair, catcher Pepper Bassett would throw out runners trying to steal second. The Indianapolis Clowns, the Harlem Globetrotters of their day, acted out a pantomime trick called shadow ball. In the 1950s, the Clowns hired three women players: Lyle "Toni" Stone, Connie Morgan, and Mamie "Peanut" Johnson. High jinks aside, the Indianapolis Clowns played serious ball. Other clown teams included the Ethiopian Clowns, Zulu Cannibal Giants, and Florida Hoboes.

Toni Stone
Female 2nd Baseman of
Negro American League
CLOWNS

King Tut, Oscar Charleston, and Connie Morgan, who played basketball during the off-season.

Hammer, grand slam, mighty swing.
Hank hits like a home run king.

Louisville Slugger issued a limited edition bat in honor of Henry Aaron and his record-breaking 715 home runs.

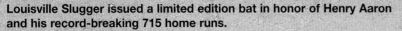

Henry "Hank" Aaron

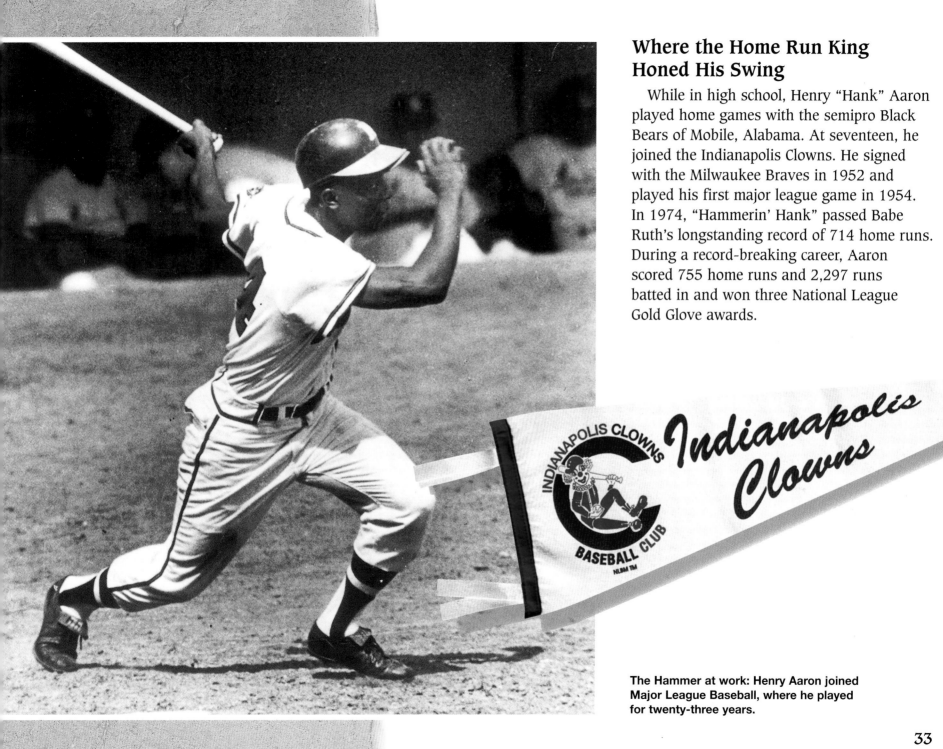

Where the Home Run King Honed His Swing

While in high school, Henry "Hank" Aaron played home games with the semipro Black Bears of Mobile, Alabama. At seventeen, he joined the Indianapolis Clowns. He signed with the Milwaukee Braves in 1952 and played his first major league game in 1954. In 1974, "Hammerin' Hank" passed Babe Ruth's longstanding record of 714 home runs. During a record-breaking career, Aaron scored 755 home runs and 2,297 runs batted in and won three National League Gold Glove awards.

The Hammer at work: Henry Aaron joined Major League Baseball, where he played for twenty-three years.

Triple-headers last past dusk.
Ride on, barnstorm, rumbly bus.

The Pittsburgh Crawfords pose in front of their custom-built tour bus.

"In addition to our regular league games, we'd barnstorm a lot. That means we'd play exhibition games in one city one day and in another city the next."

—Cool Papa Bell

Barnstorming

Most Negro League home games were held in stadiums rented from major or minor league clubs. This resulted in a short regular season of sixty to seventy games—not enough ticket sales to keep a team afloat. Negro League teams played up to 125 more nonleague barnstorming games—doubleheaders, tripleheaders, and sometimes quadruple headers—against black and white semipro and amateur teams. They even played major league teams during the off-season. These exhibition games drew both black and white fans.

On a Canadian tour in the 1930s, the Kansas City Monarchs pose with two players from the House of David team organized by a religious community in Benton Harbor, Michigan.

One-lane highways, blackjack, jokes, Saltines, sardines, root beer, Cokes.

PORK CHOP & EGGS
BACON & EGGS
HAMBURGER STEAK & EGGS
SAUSAGE & EGGS
SHORT RIBS & MACARONI 2
BEEF STEW & RICE 2
EGGS & G
HOT CAKES 15
HASH & RICE

Rural stores and gas stations, such as this one in Melrose, Louisiana, were familiar sights to players on the road.

"We logged thirty thousand miles one summer."
—Buck Leonard

A Rough Road

Touring by bus, players passed time playing cards, cracking jokes, and singing songs. But life on the road was not all fun and games. In the segregated South, players could not use white-only restrooms or drinking fountains, stay at white-only hotels, or eat at white-only restaurants. Sometimes, the players ate sandwiches on the bus. If a town had no black hotel, the players slept in black-owned boarding houses, black residents' homes, on the bus, or under the stars.

Segregation in the South was legalized with statutes called Jim Crow laws. The laws created separate facilities for whites and blacks, such as roadside cabins and water fountains.

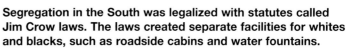

East-West contest, all-star teams.
Sweat-drenched players; diamond gleams.

Cracker Jack
popcorn confection

"THE MORE YOU EAT
THE MORE YOU WANT"

Known as the East-West game, this yearly all-star competition was held each summer at Comiskey Park in Chicago. This photograph identifies some of the players in the 1939 game, including Josh Gibson at home plate. According to the notation on the photo, the attendance was around 40,000.

COMISKEY PARK 35th St. and Shields Ave.

70 6 5

SUNDAY
AUG.
16
1942
3:00 p.m.

10th Annual.. **NATIONAL COLORED
ALL ★ STAR
BASEBALL GAME
EAST vs WEST**
BOX SEAT - - $1.65
Est. Price $1.50—Tax Paid 15c

"Everybody came to that ball game."

—Buck O'Neil

Before there was all-star competition, there was the world series. In October 1924, the Kansas City Monarchs, Negro National League champions, met the Hilldale Club, Eastern Colored League champions (on right), in the first Negro World Series. The Monarchs won, 5 games to 4.

38

1937 East team

Stellar Teams

From 1933 to 1950, the Negro League East-West All-Star Games were played in Chicago's Comiskey Park. Fans, who had used ballots in black newspapers to vote for their favorite players, came from across the country. The annual games drew huge crowds—20,000 to 50,000 fans, black and white—more than most major league clubs. For several seasons, the Negro leagues held a World Series, though that was never as successful as the East-West Games.

1942 East team

Season's over; players go South to Cuba, Mexico.

Ray Dandridge, Veracruz

Jugadores del "Habana" (Players of Havana) 1—Gonzalo Sanchez, catcher. 2—Pop Lloyd, shortstop. 3—Ricardo Hernandez, outfielder. 4—Preston Hill, outfielder. 5—Grant Johnson, shortstop and second base. 6—Luis Padron, right fielder. 7—J. H. Magrinat, outfielder. 8—Carlos Moran, third base. 9—Camilo Valdes, mascot.

Martin Dihigo

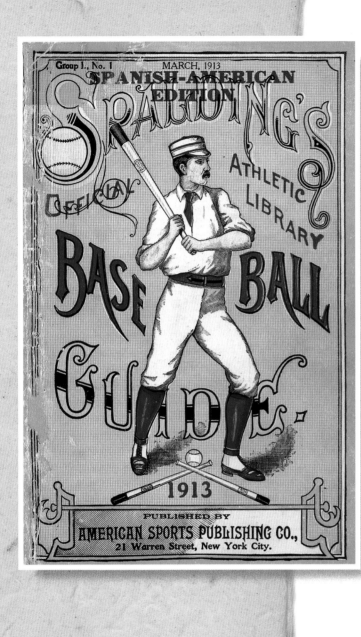

Beisbol

During the winter—off-season—many Negro League players played in Latin America, where professional baseball was not segregated. There, the African American players were treated like heroes instead of second-class citizens. In Cuba, Mexico, Puerto Rico, the Dominican Republic, and Venezuela, the players stayed at fine hotels, ate at fine restaurants, and won the hearts of fans. Several Latin American players joined the Negro League. Cuban-born pitcher Martin Dihigo is the only player inducted into the Cuban, Mexican, and United States Baseball Halls of Fame.

Josh Gibson (back row, center) playing for the Santurce team of the Puerto Rican League, along with Bill Byrd of the Baltimore Elite Giants (left) and Dick Seay (right) of the New York Black Yankees.

Jackie Robinson smacks the ball, Toppling segregation's wall.

KANSAS · CITY MONARCHS

1945 Kansas City Monarchs, with Jackie Robinson in front row, third from the left

Look magazine profiled Jackie Robinson in the November 17, 1946, issue.

Baseball's First Negro

The Dodgers sign Jackie Robinson—first breach in game's racial barrier

Branch Rickey, president of the Brooklyn Dodgers, as featured in *Look* magazine, March 19, 1946.

A Branch Grows in Brooklyn

Branch Rickey flourishes in Flatbush, champions the Negro in baseball, and is the father of major league's profitable farm system

By TIM COHANE

The Right Man to Make History

Jackie Robinson starred in football, basketball, track, and baseball at the University of California, Los Angeles. After World War II, he joined the Kansas City Monarchs. In 1945, Branch Rickey, president of the Brooklyn Dodgers, signed Robinson. Rickey made Robinson promise not to fight back when racists lashed out. On April 15, 1947, Robinson, then twenty-eight, played his first major league game. He had broken baseball's color barrier. He was National League rookie of the year in 1947 and named most valuable player in 1949. His 197 stolen bases were the most in the major leagues from 1947 to 1956. In his ten years with the Dodgers, the team won six pennants and the World Series.

Louisville Slugger issued a Jackie Robinson bat.

Jackie Robinson in action.

43

Top-notch athletes reach the goal.
Majors open; Negro Leagues fold.

Elston Howard

Sam Jethroe

The First Blacks on Major League Teams

Player	Major League Club	Date
Jackie Robinson	Brooklyn Dodgers	April 15, 1947
Larry Doby	Cleveland Indians	July 5, 1947
Hank Thompson	St. Louis Browns	July 17, 1947
Willard Brown	St. Louis Browns	July 17, 1947
Monte Irvin	New York Giants	July 27, 1949
Sam Jethroe	Boston Braves	April 18, 1950
Orestes "Minnie" Minoso	Chicago White Sox	May 1, 1951
Bob Trice	Philadelphia Athletics	September 13, 1953
Gene Baker	Chicago Cubs	September 14, 1953
Ernie Banks	Chicago Cubs	September 14, 1953
Curt Roberts	Pittsburgh Pirates	April 13, 1954
Tom Alston	St. Louis Cardinals	April 13, 1954
Nino Escalera	Cincinnati Reds	April 17, 1954
Carlos Paula	Washington Senators	September 6, 1954
Elston Howard	New York Yankees	April 14, 1955
John Kennedy	Philadelphia Phillies	April 22, 1957
Osvaldo "Ossie" Virgil	Detroit Tigers	June 6, 1958
Elijah "Pumpsie" Green	Boston Red Sox	July 21, 1959

"The success of the players who went from the Negro League to the majors proves how good the Negro Leagues were."

—Willie Mays

As teams integrated, black fans attended major league games. Faced with declining attendance, the Negro Leagues shut down after the 1963 season—but not before several black stars signed with major league clubs. Six of the first seven National League rookies of the year hailed from the Negro leagues.

Hank Thompson

Minnie Minoso

Monte Irvin and Larry Doby

Bronze their portraits, etch their names Upon a wall at the Hall of Fame.

OSCAR McKINLEY CHARLESTON

NEGRO LEAGUES 1915 - 1944

RATED AMONG ALL-TIME GREATS OF NEGRO LEAGUES. VERSATILE STAR BATTED WELL OVER .300 MOST YEARS. SPEED, STRONG ARM AND FIELDING INSTINCTS MADE HIM STANDOUT CENTER FIELDER. LATER MOVED TO FIRST BASE. ALSO MANAGED SEVERAL TEAMS DURING 40 YEARS IN NEGRO BASEBALL.

ANDREW (RUBE) FOSTER

RATED FOREMOST MANAGER AND EXECUTIVE IN HISTORY OF NEGRO LEAGUES. ACCLAIMED TOP PITCHER IN BLACK BASEBALL FOR NEARLY A DECADE IN EARLY 1900s. FORMED CHICAGO AMERICAN GIANTS IN 1911 AND BUILT THEM INTO MIDWEST'S DOMINANT BLACK TEAM. IN 1920 HE ORGANIZED NEGRO NATIONAL LEAGUE. HEADED LEAGUE AND MANAGED CHICAGO TEAM UNTIL RETIREMENT FOLLOWING 1926 SEASON.

Hall of Famers from the Negro League

Player	Position	Year Inducted
Hilton Smith	Pitcher	2001
Norman "Turkey" Stearnes	Center Field	2000
Joseph "Smokey Joe" Williams	Pitcher	1999
Wilber "Bullet Joe" Rogan	Pitcher	1998
Larry Doby	Center Field	1998
Willie "The Devil" Wells	Shortstop	1997
William Hendrick "Bill" Foster	Pitcher	1996
Leon Day	Pitcher	1995
Ray Dandridge	Third Base	1987
Henry "Hank" Aaron*	Right Field	1982
Andrew "Rube" Foster	Pitcher	1981
Willie Mays*	Center Field	1979
John Henry "Pop" Lloyd	Shortstop	1977
Martin Dihigo	Pitcher	1977
Ernest "Ernie" Banks*	Shortstop	1977
Oscar Charleston	First Base	1976
William Julius "Judy" Johnson	Third Base	1975
James "Cool Papa" Bell	Center Field	1974
Monford "Monte" Irvin*	Left Field	1973
Walter "Buck" Leonard	First Base	1972
Joshua "Josh" Gibson	Center Field	1972
Leroy "Satchel" Paige*	Pitcher	1971
Roy Campanella*	Catcher	1969
Jackie Robinson*	Second Base	1962

*Players who went on to the major leagues

Index